Original title:
Words of a Holy Night

Author: Sophia Kingsley

ISBN HARDBACK: 978-9916-90-840-2
ISBN PAPERBACK: 978-9916-90-841-9

Chants of a Softly Falling Snow

The snowflakes dance, a swirling show,
On rooftops sly, they like to sow.
A frosty fluff, a coat for each car,
While squirrels plot to steal a snack from afar.

With hats askew and mittens lost,
They trip and tumble, what a cost!
The snowman grins, a carrot nose,
As laughter bubbles, and joy just flows.

Mystical Revelations in Nocturnal Stillness

The moon whispers secrets to the trees,
While owls hoot jokes carried on the breeze.
Elves hide behind the snowy white,
Crafting mischief under starry light.

A squirrel steals a snowflake with glee,
Thinking it's a fancy cup of tea.
Yet every twinkle makes it all clear,
It's just a cozy, kooky time of year.

Serenity's Gift Beneath the Winter's Veil

Beneath the pines, the shadows play,
A snowball fight breaks out today.
While winter wraps the world so tight,
Kids giggle and dash, oh what a sight!

Hot chocolate spills, marshmallows too,
As laughter fills the air anew.
The calmness here is often broken,
By chatter and tales, all happily spoken.

Sacred Moments in the Veil of Night

As stars wink down with a cheeky glance,
The snowpals waddle, they take a chance.
A snow angel flops, making a scene,
While giggles ring out, sweet and serene.

With jingle bells jingling, what a delight,
The pets do a dance, adding to the night.
Under the glow of a soft street light,
Hilarity reigns on this merry night.

Mosaic of the Celestial Heart

In a sky where stars do dance,
The moon tells jokes that make us prance.
A comet sneezes, sparks all around,
While laughter echoes, joy unbound.

The night wears slippers, oh so bright,
And dreams take flight on feathered height.
A giggling breeze whispers delight,
As twinkling lights join in the flight.

The Stillness Before the Dawn

Before the sun, a yawn so loud,
The critters gossip, all so proud.
A squirrel cracks nuts with such finesse,
While sleepy stars don their new dress.

The owls on tree branches hold a show,
With acts so silly, oh, how they glow!
The hush of night wears a funny crown,
Before the day comes tumbling down.

A Tapestry of Radiant Night

A tapestry spun with giggles and glee,
Where shadows play tag, just wait and see.
Starlight tickles the moon on its throne,
As laughter spills, the night feels like home.

The planets whisper secrets, not so deep,
While playful meteors leap, not a peep.
A celestial jest, so lively and spry,
As the universe winks, oh my, oh my!

Tranquility in the Embrace of Stars

In the arms of glitter, we stumble and trip,
Where constellations share a chocolate chip.
Galaxies giggle at our sleepy grace,
As we twirl in circles, lost in space.

Time takes a break, it's all just a game,
With raucous laughter in cosmic fame.
The stars take selfies as they shine bright,
In the embrace of a whimsical night.

Upon Celestial Wings

The cat in a hat floats high,
Chasing stars across the sky.
With a wink and a purr,
He takes flight with a slur.

Sprinkled dreams on pizza pies,
Unicorns share silly sighs.
A dance-off with the moon,
In pajamas, they croon.

Midnight's Sacred Embrace

A toaster sings a midnight tune,
With waffles dancing, oh so strewn.
They whirl around in syrup glows,
As sleepy-eyed gnomes strike silly poses.

The fridge hums soft secret rhymes,
While celery plays old-school chimes.
In comfy socks, they jig and prance,
And sauerkraut joins the dance!

Light from the Silent Heavens

A comet sneezes, stars take flight,
While cookies bake, a tasty sight.
Moonbeams twirl in frosty air,
Painting giggles everywhere.

The planets wear their dainty hats,
Laughing at the dancing cats.
Even Saturn spins in glee,
While pointing at a dancing bee.

Lullabies of the Cosmic Realm

A giant potato tells a tale,
Of flying fish and a snoring whale.
They bounce on clouds of fluffy cheese,
With dancing ants that aim to please.

Shooting stars trade silly jokes,
As broccoli dons zany cloaks.
In this realm of dreams delight,
Every laughter shines so bright.

The Prayerful Silence of Stars

In the quiet of the night, they gleam,
Whispers of wishes, or so it seems.
Twinkling like laughter, oh what a sight,
One star bets another, 'I'll shine more bright!'

Cats in cloaks, they dance and prance,
Chasing moonbeams, in a mystical trance.
A comet zooms, just missed its cue,
'Was that a shooting star or Pat's lost shoe?'

Celestial Grace Intertwined

The sky is a canvas, of strange delight,
Aliens chuckle, what a funny sight.
'Pass the popcorn!' cries a nearby moon,
'Let’s see if Earthlings can dance to this tune!'

Jupiter winks at a shy little star,
'Come on, don’t hide, you’re a super car!'
Martians are googling, 'What’s a warm hug?'
While Earth takes a selfie, all snug as a bug.

The Beat of a Holy Heart

A rhythm starts, in the space so vast,
Heartbeats echo, a whimsical blast.
Hearts in orbit, spinning joy with glee,
'Hey you, can you feel this cosmic spree?'

The moon taps its foot, in a silvery glow,
While Saturn plays drums, just stealing the show.
'Two to the left and spin right on cue,'
The stars giggle softly, 'We’ll join you too!'

A Night Etched in Illumination

Light spills over, like butter on bread,
Brightening up dreams, tickling our heads.
A parade of fireflies waving their wings,
They laugh at the moon, 'Look at us bling!'

The sun's just a joke, sleeping away,
While the twilight says, 'Come out to play!'
With shadows that giggle and twirl in delight,
Oh, what a splendidly silly night!

Nocturnal Harmony of the Divine

In the stillness of the moon,
Cats gather for a tune,
Whiskers twitch, and tails entwine,
Meowing hymns, so divine.

Bats dance in a comical flight,
Chasing shadows, a silly sight,
Owls wisecrack up in the trees,
Hooting jokes on the midnight breeze.

A raccoon, dressed in a mask,
Searches bins; what a task!
While fireflies wink with delight,
Adding sparkles to the night.

The stars blink their secret schemes,
And giggle softly in our dreams,
Even the dark has its glee,
Under this cosmic symphony.

The Glow of Kindred Spirits

Moonlit candles flicker bright,
Two ghosts bicker over light,
One wants to haunt the old school,
The other says, "That ain't cool!"

Fairies giggle on a leaf,
Sharing tales of ancient grief,
But really, they're just making fun,
Of all the humans on the run.

A deer prances with flair so wide,
Trailing ants like a funny guide,
While owls roll their eyes above,
Whispering secrets, full of love.

In this realm of quirky cheer,
Laughter echoes, loud and clear,
When shadows dance with pure delight,
Magic laughs through the night.

Stars Speak in Secret Tongues

Stars convene in cosmic chat,
Discussing who's the silliest cat,
They giggle in twinkling streams,
While plotting ridiculous schemes.

Comets race on a sugar high,
One trips and whispers, "Oh, my!"
Saturn's rings play musical notes,
Even the planets, they crack jokes.

Meteor showers pull pranks on Earth,
Landing softly, filled with mirth,
A laugh here, a giggle there,
Making wishes float through the air.

Together, they weave the bright thread,
Of fun-filled stories overhead,
Each twinkle a chuckle in space,
Filling the universe with grace.

A Night of Sacred Whispers

Whispers drift through the sweet night air,
Like butterflies in a joyful flare,
Squirrels gossip, tails all a-fluff,
"What did you see? Is it enough?"

The moon rolls her eyes in delight,
As crickets chirp with all their might,
Singing ballads, a silly tune,
They're the nightlife's cartoon-filled boon.

Fireflies wink, playing tag above,
Engaged in a dance, a game of love,
While the trees sway, tickled by the breeze,
All of nature shares in the tease.

In shadows thick, laughter rebounds,
Binding souls in playful sounds,
Such is the charm of this night’s spree,
Mirth woven in the tapestry.

The Canvas of Midnight Grace

In shadows thick, the snacks appeared,
The moon looked down, all light impaired.
A cat in knock-offs walks the line,
While dreaming of some fancy brine.

The teddy bears hold midnight chats,
With popcorn bowls and acrobats.
A ghost recounts a cheesy plight,
In silence shrouded by delight.

With whispers soft and giggles spry,
They plot to steal the midnight pie.
But who could hear their secret game?
When every laugh just sounds the same!

So take a seat, join in the jest,
Where snorers snore and jesters rest.
In this odd hour, joy takes flight,
In canvas painted deep of night.

From Dusk to Dawning Light

When shadows dance and twilight sings,
A chicken clucks with jeweled rings.
The stars have braces and they shine,
While crickets 'tweet' and armadillos dine.

The sun awakes, a sleepyhead,
With toothpaste thoughts, a crusty spread.
It yawns aloud, what a bright sight,
As squirrels twerk in morning light!

With toast that burns and juice that's spilt,
The laughter flows, it's quite uphill.
Each knock-kneed puppy takes a flight,
In a parade of eggs benight.

So greet the day with silly cheer,
As dawn arrives, let giggles steer.
For in this twilight, laughter’s spark,
Is what ignites the coming arc!

Ethereal Echoes of Eternity

Whispered tales of goats on stilts,
In fields of socks and mystical quilts.
While shadows juggle glowing stars,
And cows go shopping for their cars.

A moonbeam tickles a grand old tree,
While ants perform a symphony.
Eternal echoes flip and flop,
As owls declare a joyful stop.

With laughter rich and chimneys puffed,
The kittens boast of ball games cuffed.
They serenade the sleepy night,
While fairies giggle, what a sight!

In realms where laughter reigns supreme,
Each echo paints a silly dream.
So let us join this endless spree,
And laugh out loud, come dance with me!

Communion of Quiet Souls

A squirrel prays with floppy ears,
While donuts weave in whispered cheers.
The teapot whistles songs of glee,
As mice perform their ballet spree.

In hushed communion, shadows flick,
Where wisdom hides in joking trick.
A turtle dons a crown of leaves,
As giggly gnomes play hide and tease.

With starry giggles that ignite,
The restless spirits take to flight.
They share a joke, a happy fate,
With each punchline they oscillate.

So gather ‘round, all merry souls,
In this quiet, laughter rolls.
For every giggle hides a prayer,
In midnight's magic, everywhere.

Twilight's Sacred Glimpse

In dusk's embrace, the cats conspire,
With twinkling eyes and tails on fire.
They plot their next great heist tonight,
As shadows dance in soft moonlight.

A squirrel steals a slice of cake,
While dogs just watch, for goodness' sake!
The night is full of silly schemes,
Amidst the glow of silver beams.

The stars above begin to wink,
While crickets pause, they stop to think.
Should they join in the frolicked fun?
Or stay in line, their work not done?

So here we laugh and let it flow,
Under a sky that steals the show.
In twilight's sight, the world's a quirk,
Where even darkness loves to smirk.

The Beacon of Inner Peace

A candle flickers with gentle smiles,
While mismatched socks run wild for miles.
The cat finds warmth upon my lap,
As puzzled dogs begin to nap.

The teapot whistles a high-pitched tune,
While cookies bake and chase the moon.
Inside this cozy, quiet cocoon,
We dream aloud of silly cartoons.

With every sip of chamomile,
I tackle thoughts that never stand still.
The mug feels heavy, warmth so vast,
While laughing ghosts partake in the past.

So let’s embrace this oddball bliss,
For in this moment, we can’t miss.
With giggles echoing in the night,
We toast the weirdness—what a sight!

A Palette of Quiet Reflections

In colors bright, the dreams collide,
While honest socks no longer hide.
The midnight snacks begin to call,
As giggles stretch and softly sprawl.

The fridge hums songs of sweet delights,
While dishes clash in playful fights.
Each spoon and fork possess a tune,
That sing of mischief under the moon.

With every brush, the laughter grows,
As paint spills bright in ringlet flows.
The canvas waits for tales untold,
Of secret crushes and friends so bold.

A splash of whimsy, a swirl of fun,
As tiny ghosts rehearse their run.
In gestures grand, we find our cheer,
For magic brews when friends are near.

Shadows Singing in Harmony

Beneath the trees, the shadows sway,
With whispers soft, they steal the day.
A frog hops in with silly grace,
While fireflies join the merry chase.

The owls debate with comic flair,
As raccoons dance without a care.
Each leaf a note within the score,
A melody of mischief galore.

When laughter echoes through the air,
Even the moon gets caught in snare.
It hides behind the clouds and peeks,
While shadows share their funny tweaks.

So join the choir of giggles bright,
As stars align in pure delight.
In every shadow, light prevails,
With harmony in silly tales.

Illuminated by Celestial Words

In the glow of magic moonbeams,
The cat plays chess with the old dreams.
Stars giggle, twinkling bright,
As shadows dance, what a sight!

Elves exchanging silly jokes,
While fairies munch on roasted folks.
A wise owl hoots in delight,
Mocking the silly things of night.

Comets dash with a screech and a zoom,
Creating space for giggles to bloom.
With every twinkle, the night takes flight,
In the warmth of a laugh, it feels just right.

Serenity's Reverberation in Darkness

The stillness hums a quirky tune,
Jellybeans float by a sleepy raccoon.
Pixies pop popcorn, such a fun show,
As nighttime spills dreams like melted snow.

Crickets serenade with jazzy beats,
While gnomes try on oversized feets.
Moonbeams wink at the mess they've made,
As laughter overflows, never to fade.

A blanket of night wraps round the mischief,
While sleepyheads drift, seeking their bliss.
In a cozy chaos, dreams take flight,
As silliness reigns in the calm of night.

Haloed Dreams Unveiled

Underneath the starlit mist,
Chickens argue, they must insist.
A raccoon juggles with a grin,
As the moonlight invites the fun in.

Dreams wrapped in laughter, oh so sweet,
Frogs in chorus shout ‘try our feet!’
With halos made of sparkly dust,
The night winks back, it’s a must!

Bats on bicycles whirl and glide,
Chasing shadows with laughter wide.
A whimsical night, full of delight,
As chaos reigns in this fancy flight.

From the Depths of the Night Sky

The night spills stars like chocolate sprinkles,
While sleepy heads mumble and wrinkle.
Squirrels in pajamas dance up high,
With donuts flying like dreams in the sky.

Whispers echo from the clouds above,
As hedgehogs swoon in ill-fated love.
Giggling watermelons roll on by,
Under the gaze of the glittering sky.

As laughter twinkles and swirls in glee,
Nothing’s quiet, oh can’t you see?
From the depths of night, joy takes its flight,
With the moon as our guide, we revel in light.

Secrets Beneath the Silver Moon

In shadows thick where secrets play,
A cat in boots has come to stay.
On rooftops high, he sings a tune,
Of cheese and mice beneath the moon.

The owls are hooting, birds are snoring,
While squirrels plot their midnight scoring.
With laughter echoing through the trees,
The wind whispers tales, if you please.

A raccoon dances, twirls around,
Through empty cans, a treasure found.
The moonlight glints on shiny things,
A night of fun, oh, what joy it brings!

So gather near, embrace the night,
For secrets shared bring pure delight.
With giggles trapped in the evening air,
We twirl our antics without a care.

Reverent Shadows of Twilight

The shadows stretch, they start to creep,
As crickets chirp, 'tis time for sleep.
But here we are with pies galore,
And giggles creeping through the door.

The stars begin their twinkling show,
While silly ants put on a show.
They march in line, they take a bow,
Confused, the moon looks on somehow.

In twilight’s glow, our jokes take flight,
As fireflies join in the delight.
With all our puns and laughter shared,
This sacred hour feels so well-prepared!

So raise your snacks and toast the fun,
For laughter shines where shadows run.
With hearts aglow and joy in sight,
We’ll dance until the morning light.

Sanctum of Ethereal Dreams

In a dreamy place where giggles bloom,
Pajama-clad folks gather in a room.
With pillows high and stories spun,
We share our dreams till the night is done.

A teddy bear, with glasses on,
Keeps track of time until the dawn.
With whispers soft, and snacks laid bare,
Together we hatch our midnight dare.

The clock strikes two, we start to plot,
Who can eat the most, and who cannot?
With laughter soaring like a kite,
This place of dreams feels just right.

So here's our pact, let's share it wide,
With playful hearts, we'll always glide.
For every giggle, every beam,
Is magic sewn in a midnight dream.

Celestial Murmurs of Hope

In starlit skies where laughter hums,
The squirrels dance and the owl drums.
With jesters hats and glowing feats,
The universe welcomes our silly treats.

Beneath the stars, we share our schemes,
With candy clouds and vibrant dreams.
Each twinkling light a reason to cheer,
As cosmic giggles fill the atmosphere.

A comet zooms with a playful wink,
We raise our cups, here's to the clink!
For in the night, our spirits soar,
With humor bright, we ask for more.

So take this joy, hold it tight,
Let laughter echo through the night.
With cosmic tales of silly hope,
We find our way, we learn to cope.

A Symphony of Starlight and Silence

Twinkling lights join the festive cheer,
While moonbeams dance without any fear.
A cat in a hat starts to meow,
As the stars sing tales of 'who's the best cow?'

The shadows chuckle in gleeful delight,
While snowflakes tiptoe, oh what a sight!
The trees wear tinsel, and squirrels make plans,
To feast on the cookies left out by the fans.

Laughter erupts with each silly jest,
As the night unfolds, it's a cosmic fest.
The owls all wink, wearing robes so bright,
Stirring the fun in this magical night.

Elysian Echoes in the Dark

In the stillness, a giggle takes flight,
Echoing softly under the moonlight.
Bubbles of laughter float high in the air,
While stars play poker, without a care.

A jolly old ghost forgets his own lines,
Flapping around like a bundle of vines.
The night creatures join in a whimsical tune,
That makes even the tired old raccoon swoon.

With fireflies ready to join in a prank,
The owls say 'Who?' like a curious prank.
The night is alive with joy and surprise,
As the universe grins right before our eyes.

Breath of the Blessed Night

In this moment, the stars play tag,
Shooting across like a bright, silly flag.
While crickets chirp in their comical way,
“And what’s the weather?” they seem to say.

A fluffy white cloud does a jig in the sky,
While the moon grins down, giving winks on the sly.
The trees rustle secrets, like gossiping friends,
As the evening unfolds and the laughter transcends.

Dancing shadows prance gracefully near,
While the chorus of joy fills the atmosphere.
A night of pure magic, who knew it would be,
A festival bright, draped in glee, wild and free!

A Dance of Divine Luminescence

Oh, glimmering lights in a whimsical spree,
Invite all the laughs to join in the glee.
A duo of stars starts a silly conga,
As a nearby comet yells, 'Hey, I'm gonna!'

The air is electric with giggles galore,
As moonlit poodles dance on the floor.
Nights filled with chuckles and playful delight,
Transforming the darkness, igniting the night.

Elves in the corners burst into a ballet,
While shadows do cha-chas, they’re ready to play.
Divine luminescence, a bright circus unfolds,
Underneath all the sparkles, a story retold.

Silent Echoes of the Sacred Hour

When socks go missing, oh the plight,
A festive dance in the soft moonlight.
The cat serenades with a purr so sweet,
While I stumble over a rogue piece of wheat.

The stars giggle down like old pals,
As I try to find my lost holiday vows.
The tree's all aglow, yet my brain's all 'no',
Look, there’s my sandwich, what a festive show!

The candles flicker, and shadows play,
As I chuckle at all the silly things I’ll say.
A sprinkle of magic in a soup of cheer,
With family gathered, there’s no room for fear!

With every loud laugh, we forget the rest,
My turkey's now doing an interpretive jest.
As we toast to the joy in this silly old fight,
I’d call it a win on this sacred night!

Celestial Whispers Beneath the Stars

The stars are twinkling, a cosmic prank,
Every wish I make lands in the tank.
I ask for peace, but my dog wants a snack,
Why do the wishes always hold me back?

The moon winks down, a mischievous face,
Reminding me of that last cookie race.
Between the laughter and playful snores,
I ponder if my fruitcake has open doors.

A comet zooms by, with a loud 'whoosh',
As Aunt Edna's holiday sweater goes 'swoosh'.
I sip hot cocoa, with whipped cream on top,
Listening to tales that never seem to stop.

In the backdrop of chaos, peace finds its way,
With chuckles and joy, it's a bright, silly play.
Under this vast sky, where laughter doth bloom,
I raise my mug high, in this starry room!

Midnight Prayers in the Winter's Embrace

In the still of the night, a wild thought came,
How did last year's fruitcake win the game?
With a side of frost and a dash of snow,
I whisper sweet secrets to the winter blow.

I'm thankful for socks, mismatched and bright,
And for Grandma's tales that give me a fright.
Snowflakes are giggling as they wiggle down,
While I keep searching for my lost golden crown.

The clock strikes twelve; my dog gives a bark,
As the neighbors set off a clumsy spark.
The prayers go up, in this wintery place,
With laughter and love, and a fumbled embrace.

With each jolly story, the night carries on,
I'm blessed to be here, where joy's never gone.
In the heart of the cold, while we snicker and sigh,
We wrap up the night with a twinkling eye!

Gentle Hymns of the Starlit Sky

Under this quilt of shimmering night,
I ponder the wonders, the giggles, the fright.
The carolers sing, but one dog gives chase,
Chasing each note like a runaway race.

Snowmen stand guard, with their silly grins,
Off to the side where the wildness begins.
I'm humming along, though I mix up the tune,
As the popcorn on strings starts to swoon.

Candles are glowing like fireflies bright,
While I trip on the rug and take flight.
With cocoa in hand, and laughter so free,
This starlit sky holds a world just for me.

As the night winds down, joy fills the air,
I tuck in each giggle and mischief to share.
In the glow of the stars, I find pure delight,
With gentle hymns echoing through the night!

A Tapestry of Dreams in Quiet Reflection

In the still of night, cats play chess,
With pawns of yarn, they plot and obsess.
The moon snickers, casting a glow,
As more snacks pop up from below.

A blanket fort made of old socks,
Hiding leftovers in the cardboard box.
Whispers of laughter, a giggle parade,
As fruit flies dance in a funny charade.

Moths in tuxedos throw a grand ball,
While crickets recite, trying not to fall.
The dull hum of dreams gives life to the scene,
As starry-eyed dreams twirl in between.

But wake up, my friends, it's just a ruse,
Nighttime silliness, we all must choose.
So let’s toast to naps, and the mess we create,
For laughter and joy are truly first-rate.

The Whispering Night of Tranquil Souls.

The owls had a gossip, oh what a scene,
Sharing wild tales like they've never been seen.
While teddy bears plot a midnight snack,
Mischievous dreams pile up in a stack.

Stars wear pajamas with glittering seams,
While the moon plays tricks on our wildest dreams.
Under pillows, we find treasure maps,
And pillow fights turn into giggling claps.

The tick tock of clocks gives a silly dance,
Each tock leading us into a trance.
As shadows sway, the night takes its call,
With giggles and snickers, we all have a ball.

So gather your dreams in a comfy heap,
For tonight's the night when silliness leaps.
In the whispers of laughter, we'll find our way,
In this quirky night, laughter is our play.

Whispers in the Starlit Dawn

The sun has hiccups, the horizon is bright,
As roosters gossip about the dark night.
Ducks wear hats, and frogs bring the cheer,
As dawn's comedy opens the curtain clear.

With jellybeans falling from cotton-candy skies,
Each pop is magic, a fun surprise.
A dance-off ensues with the squirrels in a spin,
While the moon waves goodbye with a silly grin.

The scent of pancakes fills the sweet air,
As socks work overtime, but no one cares.
The grass tickles toes in the warm morning sun,
In this wobbly world, we all have our fun.

So wake up, dear dreamers, let's take a chance,
Join the lively parade in a joyful dance.
For in every laugh, a secret is found,
In the starlit tales of this playful ground.

Echoes of Divine Serenity

In the giggling glow of the sneaky night,
The stars pulled pranks, oh what a sight!
A marshmallow cloud floated by with a grin,
While glimmering sprites play their violin.

The candles argued on which flame is best,
While animals giggled, all cozy and dressed.
With cinnamon whispers and warmth all around,
Each chuckle of joy is a treasure unbound.

With echoes of laughter in the whimsical air,
The night cracks a joke, forgetting our care.
As fireflies twinkle with mischievous delight,
They lead us in rhythm through the wacky night.

So here's to the tales that sweep us away,
In the echoes of silence where laughter can play.
In the warmth of this moment, let stories take flight,
As the universe chuckles, brightening the night.

Reverent Reflections on a Frosted Eve

The snowflakes dance, oh what a sight,
A carrot-nosed fellow looks quite polite.
He lost his hat in a gusty blow,
Now he’s a snowman with a frosty glow.

The rabbits giggle as they hop around,
In cozy scarves, they seem quite profound.
A squirrel’s caught stealing a shiny bell,
The jingle he makes is a sound quite swell.

Chandler the cat, on the window sill,
Dreams of catching a sleigh with great skill.
But all he catches is a snowflake kiss,
Then ponders aloud, “Is this bliss or a miss?”

So we sip our cocoa, all snug and warm,
While outside, the snowflakes continue their charm.
With giggles and laughter, we all unite,
To revel in joy on this frosted night.

Ethereal Murmurs of the Divine

Under twinkling stars, the whispers flow,
A duck thinks he's Santa, his waddle a show.
He quacks out loud on a shiny board,
"Bring me some bread, I'm the feast's reward!"

The angels giggle, a flowing gown,
As noodles float past like a parade in town.
They ponder if pasta will clear the skies,
"Extra cheese!" one suggests, to some surprise.

A tree stands tall, dressed up with flair,
It boasts of tinsel and a very round pear.
"Is this a fruit or a festive delight?
I can't quite say in this magical night."

So we dance around with joy and delight,
Chatting with critters until the moon's light.
For laughter and cheer are the best of signs,
When quirky moments flow through the pines.

Candles Flicker with Sacred Light

The candles flicker, the shadows prance,
A cat in a hat thinks it’s time for a dance.
He twirls and he swirls, but trips on a mat,
Now he’s stuck in a pose, looking quite fat.

The grand feast awaits, and oh, what a spread,
With lollipops hanging like ornaments red.
A fruitcake goes rolling, a bizarre sight,
But all of us laugh, what a whimsical night!

Some fruit in a bowl toss themselves in glee,
While giggling tomatoes spill over the tea.
“Who invited these veggies?” we all start to ask,
As pickles juggle, a festive task!

So we share our wishes, absurd and bright,
As candles flicker their warm, merry light.
In this moment of joy, we find pure delight,
With laughter and mischief, all perfectly right.

Tranquil Shadows Under a Star-Crowned Heaven

At dusk, the shadows begin to play,
An owl wears glasses, surveying the fray.
Squirrels recite with a flourish and flair,
Philosophical tales, quite the odd pair.

The moon pulls a prank on the timid bat,
“Why do you cling to that old wool hat?”
While mice in pajamas play tag in a heap,
Chasing their dreams, they take quite a leap!

With cookies and milk dancing in the breeze,
A snowman declares, “I’ll do as I please!”
He builds a snow fort, a fortress grand,
With gummy bears guarding, all perfectly planned.

So night takes its bow, laughter fills the air,
With joy and warmth, we all make a pair.
In tranquil shadows, under sparkling light,
We share our whims, and our hearts take flight.

An Overture of Sacred Silence

In the quiet, a cat starts meowing,
While wise owls hoot, and stars are glowing.
A celestial choir forgot their notes,
As spirits dance wearing festive coats.

Mice hold a meeting, with cheese as a prize,
They draft a plan, oh how they disguise!
But one little mouse found himself too stout,
He tripped on his tail, and squeaked in doubt.

The laughter of angels fills up the skies,
While two clumsy clouds try to do the splits.
A night of delight, with giggles and grins,
Sending wishes that swirl like the wind.

So join the fun beneath this great dome,
Where joy fills the air like a sweet lemon scone.
We'll toast to the night with a cup and a cheer,
For it's magical mischief that brings us all here.

Parchments of the Darkened Firmament

Under the moon, a raccoon does write,
Journals of secrets into the night.
His paw slips, and ink spills everywhere,
Leaving his thoughts in a comical scare.

Stars look down, giggling in delight,
At the antics below, it's quite a sight!
A squirrel joins in, with acorn in hand,
He's planning a party, isn't it grand?

With scribbles of tales, both wild and absurd,
Each line a laugh, it's quite the word.
Moonbeams are blushing, trying not to show,
As the raccoon's stories take quite a glow.

The night wraps around with a chuckle and sigh,
For every sweet mishap, we'll let out a cry.
So gather your friends, with dreams shining bright,
In the parchment of darkness, we'll revel tonight!

Bridges to the Infinite

In the distance, a bridge swings so high,
With slippers of laughter, they leap and they fly.
To reach the vast cosmos, they think it's a breeze,
But tripping on dreams brings them down to their knees.

A duck with a tie quacks out a tune,
While the stars take a bow, feeling quite in tune.
They wave their bright arms, but oh what a blunder,
As a comet zooms past, pulling clouds like thunder.

It's chaos and giggles, a delightful parade,
With cosmic confetti in every cascade.
The bridge wobbles under the weight of the night,
As silly socks dance in pure, frantic flight.

So here on this bridge, let's share all our dreams,
For laughter expands like infinite beams.
With joy as our compass, we dance to the end,
Creating our paths where giggles transcend.

Embraced by Heavenly Whispers

In the still of the night, the breeze starts to giggle,
As whispers of angels do an odd little jiggle.
They fly with a wink and a twirl in the air,
While teasing the moon with a fluffy white hair.

Each gust carries secrets, like pollen in spring,
Telling tales of mischief and silly little things.
With a sprinkle of stardust and a dash of delight,
They gather together, what a comedic sight!

A group of short clouds are playing charades,
Chasing their shadows, oh what escapades!
The moon's belly laughs as it passes by,
These whispers of joy echo up to the sky.

So come dance with the whispers, and laugh without care,

In the glow of the heavens, we'll float through the air.
With each giggle shared, our spirits will soar,
For laughter, my friend, opens every door.

Reflections of Hope in the Midnight Calm

In the stillness, a cat takes flight,
With dreams of tuna, oh, what a sight!
The moon chuckles, a glimmering eye,
Winking at mischief beneath the sky.

Whispers of laughter echo in the dark,
While owls debate, creating a spark.
A squirrel steals acorns, feeling so bold,
In the realm of shadows, fun stories unfold.

The night wears pajamas, striped and bright,
As stars paint smiles, what a delight!
Each twinkle is laughter, a cosmic jest,
In this midnight calm, we are truly blessed.

With cocoa and giggles, we gather 'round,
As the universe dances, joy is found.
In the quiet of night, may our hearts unite,
For the best of times often come out of sight.

Stars Sing, Souls Listen

In the deep of night, a chorus takes flight,
Stars strum on guitars, oh, what a sight!
The cosmos hums tunes, silly and sweet,
Melodies swirling, as dreams take a seat.

Moonbeams join in, dancing with glee,
A symphony echoes across land and sea.
While comets do pirouettes, bright and bold,
Even the planets can’t help but get sold.

While we clap our hands, two left feet,
Swaying with rhythm, what a funky beat!
The sky throws a party, wild and free,
With giggles of starlight, come join the spree!

Each twinkling spark, a joke or a pun,
In the realm of night, the laughter won.
As souls listen closely, to the joyous refrain,
Let’s dance in delight, as we sing with the rain.

A Night Draped in Reverence

As shadows play games, and whispers are heard,
A rabbit dons glasses, looking quite absurd.
It reads from a book filled with jokes so fine,
As the stars shine brightly, they chuckle in line.

With candles that flicker, like fireflies' flight,
The essence of humor makes everything light.
In the calm of the night, deep truths are spun,
While owls tell tales 'til the morning sun.

The air is infused with a giggling breeze,
As laughter erupts from the tops of the trees.
With aprons of dusk, and forks made of light,
The feast of good humor feels perfectly right.

In this haven of mirth, we gather for cheer,
With stories and legends that bring us near.
A night wrapped in reverence, joyful and bright,
We toast to the spirits that dance in the night.

Celestial Dreams Drift Through the Silence

In the blanket of stars, dreams start to sway,
With giggles of galaxies leading the way.
Meteors dash with tales that delight,
As the cosmos whispers, 'Let’s stay up all night!'

Nebulas fashion pajamas, fluffy and bright,
As comets play tag, dodging the light.
Each dose of starlight, a sprinkle of fun,
In the silence we hear, a night just begun.

Clouds cuddle together, a cozy affair,
As laughter meanders through crisp midnight air.
We listen for secrets in whispers of dreams,
While the moon tells jokes from its silvery beams.

With twinkling eyes, we embrace the absurd,
In the dance of the night, none shall be heard.
As every dream drifts and settles just right,
We cradle the magic that glows in the night.

Enchanted Peace in the Close of Day

In a world where shadows play,
Cats plot mischief in their ballet.
The moon's a great shiny ball,
While owls remind us of the call.

Socks lost in laundry's great mess,
Fluffy tails finding their rest.
As the stars begin to wink,
Teddy bears spill all they think.

Whispers of dreams float through the air,
Reindeer giggles everywhere!
While cocoa guides the sleepy cheer,
A jolly old man might appear.

Silly tales in cozy delight,
Comets dance in a soft flight.
For laughter wraps the starlit glow,
In this peace, we revel and grow.

The Night's Embrace and the Light Within

Fireflies hold a nightly spree,
Join them for tea, it's quite a glee!
Cactus winks under the moon,
Whispers of night make us swoon.

Pajamas on, it's quite a sight,
Time for stories, hugs so tight.
Midnight snacks made with great flair,
Chomp on cookies, here and there.

Cats tell tales of the chase,
A potted plant yet to embrace.
Laughter bubbles from every nook,
While shadows giggle in the book.

So let's dance with light and cheer,
For the oddities of night draw near!
With a sprinkle of fun and a twinkle of glee,
The heart sings merry, come join with me!

Celestial Magic of an Enchanted Evening

Stars are splashed like paint on a rack,
While critters in bandannas sneak back.
The moon laughs with a cheesy grin,
Let the shenanigans begin!

Balloons float up with a pop,
While the sun says it's time to stop.
Cucumbers dance, what a strange sight,
They party like it's Friday night.

Whimsical hats on every head,
While crickets tap dance in bed.
The night's a canvas, full of glee,
Where even the roses join the spree.

So gather all, in jolly delight,
For we're wrapped in enchantment tonight!
With socks mismatched and hearts so light,
We twirl and spin till first light.

Mysteries Revealed Under Starlit Canopy

Beneath the stars, hedgehogs plot,
Secret missions, do they trot?
With each twinkle, they take a stand,
While baby rabbits try to understand.

The moon whispers secrets so sweet,
To the dancing shadows that move their feet.
Goblins giggle, their pranks on the way,
As fireflies twinkle in a balmy sway.

A frog in glasses reads a tale,
Of broad adventures and a small snail.
Laughter echoes in the cool night air,
As dreams collide with starlight rare.

So join the feast of quirky light,
As every creature reigns in delight.
Together we'll share what we've spied,
In the mysteries where joy and silliness collide.

A Prayer in the Stillness

In the hush of the night, here I sit,
With socks mismatched, oh what a hit!
I whisper to stars, they giggle in glee,
A prayer for my cat, who slept on my knee.

The moon winks at me, dressed in bright cheese,
I chuckle and say, "Oh please, just tease!"
The owls start to hoot, a wise old tune,
As I dance with my broom in the light of the moon.

Each twinkle above, a promise of fun,
I laugh with the night, we're not yet done.
The wind joins the symphony, rustling trees,
It sounds like my fridge, a great buzzing breeze.

With each passing hour, my giggles grow loud,
I drop all my worries, I'm part of the crowd.
The stars must be laughing, their lights all aglow,
In this prayer of the silly, I'm ready to go!

Beneath the Shimmering Veil

Beneath the veil where sparkles play,
I trip on my words, oh what a display!
The comets are chuckling, my jokes all gone,
As I dance with the shadows till the break of dawn.

The angels are sipping on cosmic punch,
While I'm in a quandary with a midnight crunch.
I try to recite a verse from my heart,
But hiccups disrupt me, a colorful art.

The stars roll their eyes as I stammer and sway,
"Keep it together!" I hear them say.
But laughter erupts like confetti in flight,
As I prance in my pajamas, what a delight!

With every faux pas, the night just gets bright,
I raise up my glass to the magical sight.
So here's to the folly, the giggles, the cheer,
Under this shimmering veil, there's nothing to fear!

Chants of the Starry Sphere

On the edge of the cosmos, I start to hum,
With a voice like a kazoo, oh what a strum!
The stars start to sway, a celestial jig,
While I trip over puddles, my own little gig.

Asteroids join in with bright little spins,
A raucous parade, where mayhem begins.
My tunes are all jumbled, but who could resist,
When even the planets have joined in the twist?

With meteors flying, I dance with great flair,
While the Milky Way laughs, it's beyond compare.
Each echo of laughter waves out through the night,
As I chant to the universe, oh what a sight!

With missteps aplenty, I still feel the cheer,
For even in blunders, the stars are quite near.
In this wild celebration, we twirl and we spin,
Each chant is a joy, let the fun now begin!

Celestial Reflections of Faith

In the mirror of night, my reflection I see,
With hair like a comet, wild and free!
I strike a bold pose, as the galaxies laugh,
At my faith in the cosmos, a whimsical craft.

The universe winks, it gives quite a show,
As I dance with my doubts, oh where do they go?
With glittering stardust adorning my face,
I leap through the cosmos, in wild, joyful grace.

With hope in the air, and giggles all round,
I prance through the starlight, a joy I have found.
The planets nod softly, they know what I mean,
That faith is a dance, with each little gleam.

So beneath all the wonders, I celebrate cheer,
With antics galore, I let go of my fear.
In this cosmic mirror, we laugh and align,
For the reflections of joy are both silly and divine!

Celestial Whispers of the Soul

Stars giggle up above, bright and bold,
They twinkle and jest, secrets untold.
A comet sneezed, the sky's in a fit,
While the moon plays catch with a cosmic wit.

Planets waltz, with halos so round,
Even asteroids laugh with a clangy sound.
In this stellar fiesta, we'll dance all night,
Chasing shooting stars that tickle with light.

Cosmic confetti, what a sight to behold,
While meteor showers rain silver and gold.
Galaxies chuckle as they spin and twirl,
In the universe's jest, we all uncurl.

So let's toast with comets, and raise a cheer,
To the laughter of space, let's spread it here.
In this whimsical realm, we're never alone,
The universe winks, and we've found our home.

Midnight’s Halo of Serenity

In the depth of night, cats conspire,
Plotting their mischief, fueled by desire.
They stare at the moon like it owes them a treat,
As shadows dance lightly on nimble feet.

The owls are hooting, wise but bemused,
While fireflies flicker, a bit overused.
Each breeze brings whispers of nonsense and glee,
Nature's own stand-up—a wild comedy spree.

Creaky old trees sway with the tales they spun,
While crickets play backup to nature's fun.
Even the stars seem to chuckle aloud,
In this nighttime circus, we’re all part of the crowd.

So let’s tiptoe through dreams, with giggles in tow,
Embracing the antics that night’s creatures show.
In twilight’s embrace, where oddities blend,
We’ll rest ‘neath the laughter, our hearts will transcend.

Glimmers in the Shroud of Night

Beneath velvet skies, mischief takes flight,
Raccoons host parties that last through the night.
They steal all the snacks, but we can't dismay,
For their antics bring laughter, who needs gourmet?

The shadows play tag with the moon's silver glow,
While whispers of giggles tumble below.
A bear on a bike? Oh what a sight!
In the ballroom of night, everything feels right.

Dancing with echoes, the stars take a spin,
A cosmic rave where the night's friends begin.
With lanterns aglow and dreams in the air,
Every chuckle from nature's a joyous affair.

So let's linger awhile, in this mirthful embrace,
As we wander through wonders, no need for a race.
In the glimmers that glitter, and shadows that play,
The laughter of night wraps our spirits in sway.

Silent Songs of the Heart

Hushed tones of the night, where giggles reside,
In the heart's quiet corners, joy cannot hide.
With starlit confessions, we chatter and scheme,
As dreams string us together like a whimsical dream.

A napping old dog lets out a snore,
While the moonlight giggles, wanting more.
Each flicker of light brings a smile to share,
Even the shadows seem to dance in the air.

The whispers of night were crafted with flair,
With echoes of laughter that float everywhere.
So let's hum a tune that the crickets compose,
In this symphony of silliness, anything goes.

As the night gently sways, with secrets to grant,
We'll weave funny tales that make our hearts chant.
In the stillness we find, our spirits ignite,
With silent songs strumming through the soft night.

Hymns of the Cosmic Choir

In the dark, the stars all twirled,
Singing tunes, a cosmic world.
Aliens danced in silver gowns,
While comets laughed and spun around.

A moonbeam slipped upon a shoe,
And winked as if it really knew.
Galaxies clapped with a boom,
As Saturn's rings went 'zoom zoom zoom!'

The asteroids played a rugged beat,
While planets tripped on dancing feet.
A supernova popped with cheer,
“Get up! It’s party time, my dear!”

So here we are, beyond the night,
Wobbling stars give us delight.
In laughter's glow, we’ll sing away,
The oddity of our cosmic play.

A Whisper Beneath the Cosmos

Whispers drift through the cosmic sea,
A giggle from Orion, just for me.
The moon cracked jokes with a sly disguise,
While Venus rolled her twinkling eyes.

A star fell down and said, “Hello!”
I tripped on stardust, just to show.
Shooting stars shared secrets bright,
A cat's meow echoed through the night.

“A cosmic dance?” the sun did shout,
As little comets spun about.
Neptune giggled with a bubbly burst,
“It’s not just stars, it's the universe!”

So, let’s laugh beneath the skies,
With twinkling dreams that never die.
In the dark, we find our light,
With whispers of the cosmic night.

Illuminated Paths of Tranquility

On paths aglow, the stars do gleam,
Each shimmer holds a funny dream.
A rabbit hopped, his ears so wide,
As Jupiter chuckled from his ride.

The Milky Way spilled its cosmic tea,
"Grab a cup, come dance with me!"
Satellites played a game of tag,
While meteors flew, they laughed and bragged.

In this glow, we can't complain,
As starlight dances down the lane.
Uranus rolled in giggles true,
"Life's just better when you undo!"

Let's frolic on these paths tonight,
With laughter ringing, pure delight.
The universe, it holds a charm,
Just take a step, and you'll disarm.

Lilt of the Night's Secret

The night has secrets all to share,
Like socks that vanish unaware.
A whisper giggles, "What a plight!"
As stars twinkle with pure delight.

A cosmic giggle fills the air,
As suns spin tales from here to there.
With every chuckle, a spark ignites,
In the vastness of the wondrous nights.

A nebula danced a belly shake,
While crickets chirped for heaven's sake.
"Join us, friend!" called the starlit crew,
"Let's sip on stardust, just me and you!"

In this lilt, we find our peace,
With a galaxy's laugh, our joys increase.
So spin with me and take a flight,
In the humor of the cosmic night.

Serene Voices of the Nighttime Glow

In the stillness, cats hold court,
Debating snacks of fish and pork.
The stars above just twinkle bright,
While owls hoot during their nightly flight.

Mice in tuxedos dance with glee,
Chasing shadows, so carefree.
The moon laughs softly, all aglow,
As crickets join the midnight show.

A fox sings to the sleeping trees,
Praising night with all its ease.
They toss around their funny dreams,
Where nothing's ever as it seems.

So tiptoe through this joyful maze,
Where silliness turns night to days.
The gentle breeze is in on it too,
Whispering secrets that feel brand new.

Lullabies of the Moonlit Sanctuary

Bunnies wear pajamas, soft and bright,
While fireflies twirl in sheer delight.
The stars peek in like curious friends,
To watch the night’s laughter never ends.

A bear in slippers, tiptoeing around,
Humming tunes with a sleepy sound.
He trips over his big fluffy paws,
And giggles softly, finding his flaws.

The owls play cards, shouting out “Boo!”
While the raccoons offer chips and stew.
Even the nightingales join the fun,
Singing lullabies until the night’s done.

As the moon grins, it hugs the trees,
Encouraging chuckles on the breeze.
In this sanctuary, pure delight,
Everyone's happy in the moonlit night.

Divine Conversations in the Stillness

The angels gather for some tea,
Discussing things we cannot see.
With cupcakes shaped like clouds and stars,
They giggle over sweet bizarre bars.

Saints exchange tales of silly sins,
Where laughter fuels their holy spins.
With jokes about a fallen shoe,
They find redemption in humor too.

Celestial beings, dressed in white,
Trade wisecracks on a breezy night.
As planets spin tales of their own,
Creating laughter far from the throne.

The night listens with a joyful heart,
To the hilarious tales that will never part.
In cosmic laughter, they find the key,
To light the universe, eternally free.

Graceful Echoes of a Celestial Time

Under starlight, clowns parade,
With painted faces, unafraid.
They tumble and roll across the sky,
Making even comets laugh as they fly.

In cosmic parks, the rockets race,
While aliens grin in a funny embrace.
They've traded in their space suits for jokes,
To play with the Earthlings and tickle their throats.

Galaxies twirl in a dance of cheer,
As laughter ricochets, far and near.
The universe chuckles, a grand old time,
Echoing joy in rhythm and rhyme.

So join the party, lift your gaze,
To find the humor in cosmic ways.
For in this moment, silliness climbs,
Echoing through the graceful chimes.

The Celestial Promise of Peace

In the hush of the moon, cats gather round,
Chasing their tails with the oddest sound.
The stars blink down like they're winking at you,
While the owls gossip over the latest brew.

Beneath the blanket of velvet so wide,
Squirrels dance nervously, filled with pride.
In this strange hour where dreams take a flight,
Even the puppies are howling with delight.

A shooting star falls, landing flat on the lawn,
Causing a ruckus, it makes quite the yawn.
It stretches and sighs, 'Ah, what a journey!'
Hopscotch in the cosmos, ain't that quite funny?

And as the night grins with a mischievous gleam,
The moon spins tales in a soft, silver beam.
Remember, dear friends, when the night greets the day,
It's laughter that carries our worries away.

Woven Threads of Night's Embrace

In the garden of shadows, odd things do creep,
The crickets and frogs hold a meeting of sheep.
With a chorus of giggles that rises and floats,
As the stars wish upon the gossipy goats.

Under the blanket of a starlit parade,
A raccoon in a mask plans an epic charade.
Juggling moonbeams and laughing with glee,
His tiny paw slips, oh what a sight to see!

The fireflies twinkle like tiny bright sprites,
Dancing in circles, they win all the fights.
As the night wears on, all quarrels are done,
In this chaotic blend of the moon’s silver fun.

So here’s to the night, wrapped in laughter and cheer,
A simple reminder of why we hold dear,
The moments we share in this wacky old dance,
Where silliness blooms, like a comedic romance.

A Night Dripped in Celestial Ink

In a sky full of giggles, the planets align,
An octopus winks with a sparkle so fine.
Under starlit chandeliers, owls take the lead,
While the squirrels recite silly poems with speed.

The comets are gossiping, making quite fuss,
About a pizza that fell from the celestial bus.
A raccoon sips cocoa, wearing a tie,
While the stars burst out laughing, oh my, oh my!

Clouds drift by, each sporting a grin,
As the night unravels, let the laughter begin.
A hedgehog rolls by in a sparkly coat,
Winking at bunnies, fueling their hope.

So raise up your voices and jingle your toes,
For this canvas of night's where the bright humor flows.
In this jester's cosmos, let's laugh through the fray,
With sparkle and joy, we'll dance till the day.

The Reverie of Infinite Starlight

In the twilight's embrace, stories take flight,
A snail plays the piano, it's quite the sight.
With a rhythm so slow, it grooves to the beat,
While the stars tap their feet, oh what a treat!

A tiny asteroid rides a comet's tail,
Sipping stardust smoothies, leaving a trail.
A butterfly waits for the moon to play muse,
In a twinkling gala, it's a colorful fuse.

Balloons made of galaxies bounce through the air,
While marshmallows float without worry or care.
As laughter erupts from this whimsical scene,
Even the galaxies know how to glean.

So let's join the party, take a swing and a twirl,
Under the cosmic disco, give the stars a whirl.
With joy in our hearts, loud giggles we'll share,
For in this tapestry, let humor declare!

Milton Keynes UK
Ingram Content Group UK Ltd.
UKHW020908291124
451807UK00013B/804

9 789916 90841